Stolen Dreams

David Parker
Dec 4, 1997

Portraits
of
Working
Children

Stolen Dreams

by David L. Parker with Lee Engfer and Robert Conrow
Photographs by David L. Parker

Lerner Publications Company · Minneapolis

For Mary, whose love and support helped make this book possible. For those who work for justice and human rights. Above all, for the children who have never had an opportunity to play in the sun.

Acknowledgments
The following photographs and illustrations are reproduced courtesy of: page 6, Corbis-Bettmann; page 9, Reuters/Jim Bourg/Archive Photos; page 15, AP/Wide World Photos; page 54, Archive Photos; pages 97 and 98, Tom Gorman. The map on pages 24–25 is by Laura Westlund. The quote on page 99 by Albert Shanker appeared in his column entitled "A School for Iqbal" in the *New York Times,* September 22, 1996, copyright Albert Shanker, and is used here with permission. Book design by Zachary J. Marell.

LIBRARY OF CONGRESS CATALOGING-IN-PUBLICATION DATA

Parker, David L. (David Lewis), 1951–
   Stolen dreams : portraits of working children / by David L. Parker
with Lee Engfer and Robert Conrow; photographs by David L. Parker.
    p. cm.
   Includes bibliographical references and index.
   Summary: Photographs and text document working children especially in Nepal, India, Bangladesh, and Mexico. Includes a chapter on Iqbal Masih, the child labor activist from Pakistan.
   ISBN 0-8225-2960-2 (alk. paper)
   1. Children—Employment—Juvenile literature. 2. Children—Employment—Case studies—Juvenile literature. [1. Children—Employment.] I. Engfer, LeeAnne, 1963– . II. Conrow, Robert, 1942– . III. Title.
HD6231.P37 1998
331. 3'1—dc21   97-4939

Manufactured in the United States of America
1 2 3 4 5 6 – JR – 03 02 01 00 99 98

CONTENTS

Child labor in the textile industry, Fall River, Massachusetts, 1912.
Photograph by Lewis Hine.

PREFACE

DURING THE INDUSTRIAL ERA in the United States, the growing need for labor drew the youngest of workers into the labor force. Without safety provisions or fresh air, children were forced to work long hours for little compensation. The pale, gaunt face of the child worker was brought to the attention of the American people not only by labor leaders like Samuel Gompers but by writers such as Upton Sinclair and photographers such as Lewis Hine.

Over the past five years, I have photographed children working in a variety of occupations in the United States, Mexico, Thailand, Nepal, Bangladesh, Indonesia, and India. The focus of my photography has grown out of my work as an occupational health physician. Five years ago, I began to study the effects of work on the health of young workers in Minnesota. I was surprised to find almost no information about the health problems affecting young workers in the United States.

Like many people, I thought that child labor had largely disappeared. I did not realize that more than 250 million children worldwide still work to sustain basic needs of food, clothing, and a place to live. Many of these children live on the street. Some are held as slave workers, and others scavenge food on the street and in garbage dumps. Few have the chance to go to school.

I have been encouraged by the wonderful efforts of so many children who are working to alleviate the problem of child labor. Around the world, kids are organizing to build schools; they are boycotting items that are made by children; they are saying they will not support the abuse of other children.

I hope the photographs in this book will inspire the viewer to ask questions. When should children work? How should we decide what we will allow children to do? What role should governments play in stopping child labor? What alternatives are open to children who work?

Above all, I hope that my photographs serve as witness to a shameful problem in the history of the world and as a source of encouragement to those who are working hard to end the abuse of others.

David L. Parker

the
story
of
IQBAL MASIH

Weaver
Kathmandu, Nepal

EACH MORNING, six days a week, more than half a million children between the ages of four and fourteen rise before dawn and make their way along dark country roads leading to Pakistan's carpet factories. Most of these children must be at work by 6:00 A.M. If they are late, they may be punished—hit with a wooden cane, or worse, hung upside down, their ankles tightly bound with rope. The carpet weavers work 14 hours a day, with only a 30-minute break for lunch.

Iqbal Masih was one of these workers. He started working in a carpet factory when he was just four years old. His parents were poor farmers living near Lahore, the largest city in Pakistan. Because they did not have enough money to feed their children or buy them clothes, Iqbal's parents made a very difficult choice. In exchange for a small sum of money, about $16, they agreed to send their son to work in a nearby carpet factory until he had earned enough money to pay back the loan. Iqbal was told he would be paid three cents a day for his work.

A man named Arshad owned the factory. Inside, the only light came from two bare light bulbs that hung in the middle of the room like dragon's eyes. Only a few flecks of paint dotted the walls. The carpet looms looked as though they were a hundred years old. Two strong wooden beams ran across the top and bottom of each loom's frame, which had been created by driving four large stakes into the ground.

In front of each loom sat a small child on a piece of wood scaffolding. The young weaver would tie short lengths of brightly colored thread to a warp of heavier white threads. To make just one carpet, workers had to tie more than a million small knots into a colorful rhythm of circles, squares, and other intricate designs. In the United States, hand-knotted carpets such as these sell for more than $2,000 each.

The scaffold bench could be moved up or down as the child worked on the rug, so the rug did not have to be moved. Except for a rare and forbidden whisper, the children never spoke to one another. "If I let them talk, I know they will start making mistakes," Iqbal's boss said. "And when they make mistakes, I lose money."

If the children complained about how they were treated, they were beaten. Over the years, Iqbal received many cuts and bruises from Arshad's punishments. And Iqbal found out what would happen if he talked back or tried to force Arshad to stop treating the workers so badly.

One night, when Iqbal was 10 years old, Arshad pulled him out of bed at 3:00 A.M. and ordered him to repair some carpets. Iqbal went to the local police to complain. He told them that his boss had beat him up and showed them the bruises on his arms. One of the police officers glared at Iqbal. He told him he had no right to complain— he'd better stick to his work and do what he was told. The officer grabbed Iqbal by his sore arm and led him back to the factory. "If he tries this again, chain him to his loom," the officer told Arshad.

Arshad did chain Iqbal to his loom. Even when Iqbal hurt so much he could hardly move, he fought back. He believed that what Arshad was doing was wrong.

At 10 years old, Iqbal was just under 4 feet tall, the normal size of a child who is two or three years younger. He weighed less than 60 pounds. From years of sitting hunched in front of the loom, his spine curved like that of an old man. When Iqbal walked, his feet shuffled slowly, as though he were wearing slippers that were too big.

Arshad told Iqbal that the harder he worked, the faster the loan made to his parents would be paid off. But no matter what Iqbal did, the loan just got bigger and bigger. Iqbal's father left home, and his mother was forced to borrow more money from Arshad. By the time Iqbal was 11 years old, his loan had increased to $419—more than 25 times the original amount. When Iqbal heard this, he knew he would be trapped forever unless he found a way to escape.

In the summer of 1992, Iqbal heard about a meeting to be held in a nearby town. A man named Essan Ulla Khan was going to speak about a new law forbidding carpet factories to employ children. Iqbal decided he must go to this meeting.

On the day of the meeting, Iqbal had worked almost 16 hours. In Arshad's factory there were no fans and no open windows. In the summer, the heat climbed to 120 degrees Fahrenheit. When Iqbal finally made it to the meeting, he was exhausted and very hot. He managed to push his way through the crowd to the front. He sat on the floor below the platform where Khan was speaking.

Khan talked about an organization called the Bonded Labor Liberation Front (BLLF). Its goal was to free Pakistan's bonded laborers. Like Iqbal, they were treated as slaves. The companies they worked for owned them just as they owned property or buildings. The workers were not free to leave their jobs. Khan said that thousands of children worked in bondage in Pakistan's textile and brick factories, tanneries, and steelworks. Under the new law, bonded laborers did not have to work if they did not want to.

When Khan finished speaking, several people jumped up to ask questions. Finally Khan noticed Iqbal's small raised hand and told the audience to let the boy speak. After

For many children working under harsh conditions, Iqbal Masih provided a voice. He gave them the courage to follow him out of bondage.

a pause, Iqbal asked quietly, "How can I stop working and go to school?" Khan explained that Iqbal had new rights under the law. He could show Arshad some legal papers and Arshad would have to let Iqbal go. Khan also told Iqbal about the schools that the BLLF sponsored for children who had been bonded laborers.

The next morning, when Iqbal returned to the carpet factory, he took the legal papers with him. He told Arshad he would no longer work, nor would he pay his debt, because bonded labor was illegal. Arshad's face grew red with anger. He cursed at Iqbal and beat him. But Iqbal escaped and ran out of the factory.

Two days later, Arshad came to Iqbal's home, demanding that Iqbal return to the factory or pay the money he said the family owed. Iqbal stood his ground. He knew he could count on his new friend for help.

Khan did help Iqbal get away from the factory. He threatened to have Arshad arrested if he protested. Khan greatly admired Iqbal's courage and perseverance. He found Iqbal a place in a BLLF primary school in Lahore.

Iqbal told his teachers that he wanted to become a lawyer and fight for children's rights. He did not want any child to suffer the way he had. Some of the other kids at school teased him by calling him "Chief Justice," but he didn't care. He worked hard at school and was a good student. Every night after school, he brought a book to bed and read late into the night.

Other children were not as lucky. Many did not hear about the new law. Factory owners kept workers from talking to people from the BLLF. The police did not enforce the labor law, and factories just ignored it.

Iqbal and Khan started traveling together to talk about the new law and to free young bonded laborers. One day Khan took Iqbal to visit a carpet factory in a village called Kasur. Because Iqbal was so small, the guards let him in the gate, thinking he was just another worker. But once he was inside, Iqbal started asking the children questions. How often were they beaten? How often did they have to work overtime? How were they treated?

Khan used the information that Iqbal gathered to write an investigative report.

Iqbal Masih received a Reebok Human Rights Award in 1994.

Because of the report, police raided the factory and found 300 children who had been tortured and beaten. They were all between the ages of four and ten.

When Iqbal was 12 years old, he began speaking to huge crowds in Pakistan and India. He inspired 3,000 child workers to break away from their masters. He encouraged adults to demand better working conditions. People in Europe and the United States heard about Iqbal and invited him to come speak in their countries. He told audiences that the colorful carpets some of them had in their homes were made by children who lived as slaves. In the United States, Iqbal was featured on ABC News as "Person of the Week." The Reebok Corporation honored him with an award for his work.

Carpet weaver
Rajasthan, India

Appliqué workers, Rajasthan, India

When people learned how their carpets were being made, they did not want to buy any more. In 1992, factories in Pakistan sold fewer carpets to foreign countries than in previous years. At first, the decline was slight, but two years later sales fell sharply.

Carpet factory owners and managers were furious. The Pakistan Carpet Manufacturers and Exporters Association blamed "subversive organizations" and "the child revolutionary." Threats were made on Iqbal's life.

On Easter Sunday in 1995, Iqbal went to visit relatives in a rural village. After spending some time with his aunt, he and two cousins rode their bicycles to see Iqbal's uncle, who was working in a nearby field. As the boys bounced along the dirt path, someone suddenly fired a shotgun at them from a short distance. Iqbal was instantly killed. He was 12 years old.

No one knows exactly what happened or who killed Iqbal. Some people say it was an accident. Others say it was a murder arranged by the carpet manufacturers. The real facts may never be known. Many human rights groups accused the police of failing to investigate the crime thoroughly.

At Iqbal's funeral, 800 mourners crowded into the small village cemetery. A week later, 3,000 protesters—half of them under the age of 12—marched through the streets of Lahore. For many children working under harsh conditions, Iqbal Masih provided a voice. He gave them the courage to follow him out of bondage. His story brought attention to the plight of the world's working children.

kids

at

WORK

Brick factory
Kathmandu, Nepal

NEARLY 250 MILLION CHILDREN around the world work, according to the International Labour Organisation (ILO). What does that mean? How old are these children? What kinds of work do they do? Different cultures view childhood in different ways. In some places, you might be considered an adult at age 12. You could get married or start learning a trade, such as farming or wood carving. In another place, a nine-year-old can become an apprentice, learning a useful skill from an adult worker.

Most people around the world agree, however, that certain kinds of work and working conditions hurt a child. Child labor is defined as the use of children under 16 years old for work that is harmful to their health, education, and development. Child labor doesn't include helping out with household chores or a family business unless this work keeps a child from attending school. Work is considered harmful when a child starts full-time work at too young an age, works too many hours, or when the work is so hard that it hurts the child's body or spirit.

Aarti is seven years old and works in a brick factory in the Kathmandu Valley of Nepal. Scattered throughout Nepal and India are thousands of these factories. They make bricks that are used for building homes and factories. Even a small factory produces more than a million bricks a year. Each brick is made by hand.

Brickworkers
Kathmandu, Nepal

Aarti works eight to ten hours a day with her father. She began working at the factory after her mother died.

Making bricks takes several steps. First, Aarti's father and other workers dig layers and layers of thick red clay from the earth. They knead the muddy clay until it's soft enough to be molded into a brick. To make a brick, Aarti sprinkles sand into a brick mold (an empty case in the shape of a brick) so the mud won't stick to the mold. Next she scoops up a handful of mud and throws it into the mold. She cuts the extra mud from the top with a piece of wire, then taps the mold on the ground to shape the brick. She quickly flips the mold over, turning the brick onto the ground. It will dry in the hot sun before it is fired (baked) in the brick kiln, or oven. Repeating these motions over and over under the glare of the hot sun,

Brickworker
Kathmandu, Nepal

Aarti makes between 1,000 and 1,500 bricks each day.

The whole area where Aarti works is gray with dust and smoke. Thick black smoke bellows from the kiln's chimneys. There is no fresh water, only a dirty pond. One-room brick huts, where the workers live, are scattered around the area. In Aarti's hut, Aarti and her father and sister sleep on the dirt floor. Twice a day she gets a meal of lentils and rice—sometimes it's only rice.

Aarti and other children who work at the brick factories are not healthy. They have stomach problems, coughs, body aches, eye and finger injuries, and bruises. They are at risk of developing lung diseases.

WHERE DO CHILDREN WORK ?

In some countries, kids have enough to eat, can attend school, and have time to play. Other children are not so fortunate. Around the globe, from one end of the earth to the other, kids get up in the morning and go to work. Most working children live in less developed countries—places where countless numbers of people barely have enough money to survive. In these nations, almost 25 percent of children between the ages of 5 and 14 work. That's more than two out of every ten children.

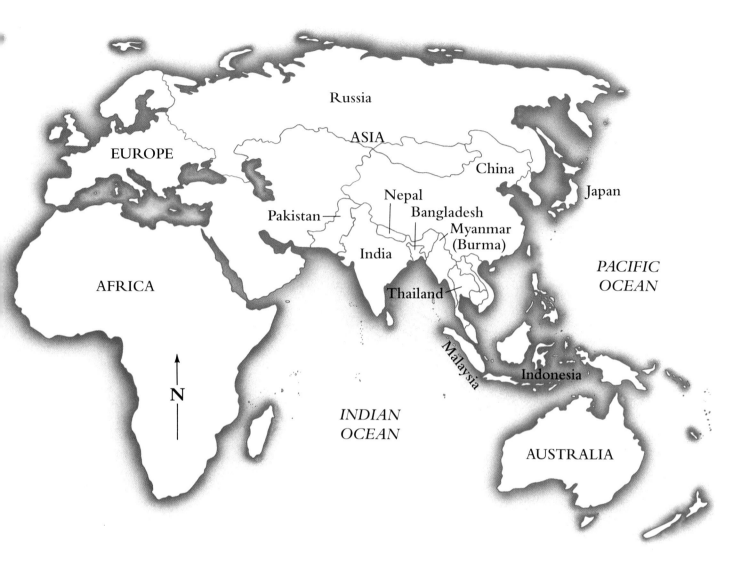

The areas where the most children work are Africa, Asia, and Central and South America. India has the largest child labor force in the world, with somewhere between 20 and 80 million children working.

In Pakistan, despite laws forbidding child labor, the number of working children is estimated at 11 to 12 million—one-fourth of the total work force. In China, as many as 12 million children work full time.

In the United States, many adolescents work—two-thirds of high school juniors and three-fourths of seniors. By comparison, only 2 percent of teenagers in Japan, another industrialized nation, work outside the home.

While most teens in the United States work legally, many young people are employed illegally. For example, many children work in sweatshops in urban garment districts. Sweatshop is a name given to any business that often violates laws on wages, hours, child labor, and occupational health and safety. In the U.S., sweatshops are found in the clothing and meatpacking industries, as well as restaurants and grocery stores.

Carnival worker
St. Paul, United States

Construction worker
Bangkok, Thailand

A Migrant Farmworker
Tells Her Story

My name is Belinda Quintanilla. Three years ago, at the age of 11, I started working in the fields picking squash and bell peppers at different farms. Each summer, my family migrates from Mission, Texas, to the eastern shore of Maryland. The worst part about migrating is having to adjust everywhere I go, even if I don't like it. Since my first year in school I have had to change schools twice a year. Because I like to read, changing schools has not affected my education too much.

It is terrible working in the fields. I work alongside my parents under the sun, huffing and puffing and aching everywhere. Sometimes there is no clean water available to help quench our thirst, and most of the time there is no water for washing our hands and faces before eating or after going to the bathroom.

For me, there is no such thing as a summer vacation. Once school is out, we pack our things and head to Maryland to find work. We have to work every single day when work is available, even if it is 90 degrees or raining. Instead of going home while it rains, we wait under the trees to see if the rain will pass. We have to work because we need the money.

It is very dangerous to work in the fields because of all the pesticides that are used to control insects. On the very first day of work this season I developed a rash all over my legs. The rash made my legs very red and itchy. But even so I went to work the next day.

Picking squash gets easier day by day, but the pay is low. I have to pick at least 60 buckets to make it worthwhile. A full bucket weighs about 25 pounds. By the way, I don't eat squash because it reminds me of working in the fields.

Although American farmworking children are not bound or beaten, I feel that the loss of young minds and innocence is great. No child belongs in the field and every child deserves an opportunity to enjoy their childhood.

I would like the government to consider regulations and programs that could help children who work in the fields. I am not asking for a handout. I am simply asking for the opportunity to learn and work while helping my parents.

Silk-screen worker
Jodhpur, India

Goatherd
Rajasthan, India

WHAT KINDS OF WORK DO KIDS DO?

Children work in fields and factories, work-shops and tea shops, on deep-sea fishing platforms and construction sites, at home, and on the street. Kids sit hunched before looms, weaving carpets, straining to see in the dark. They pound bricks or stones into gravel. They make shoes and soccer balls, fireworks and matches, locks, furniture, pencils, toys, cigarettes. They weave silk and carve wood. They sew clothing. Children

*Garbage pickers
Dhaka, Bangladesh*

Fish vendor, Coonoor, India

work in scorching heat in glass factories, and they risk their lives in brickyards, mines, and quarries, where they may get lung diseases. They clean poisonous barrels of leather-tanning fluid and turn red-hot, molten brass into fanciful handicrafts that will be sold in gift shops across the world.

Kids scrounge through garbage dumps and gutters looking for bits of rags to sell and food to eat. They shine shoes. They beg.

Fishing platform worker
Sumatra, Indonesia

Street performer, Mexico City, Mexico

Circus performer
Kathmandu, Nepal

"We are reduced to the level of the horses, bears, and other animals who dance to the tune of the ringmaster of this circus company. You just can't imagine the fright and helplessness we experience when we entertain you with breathtaking feats of trapeze and jumping shows."

—Santull, a nine-year-old girl from Nepal,
rescued from a touring circus company

Kids sell newspapers and candy and trinkets and cigarettes on street corners. They sell their own bodies.

Children pick crops of all sorts—rice, broccoli, strawberries, squash, melons. They tend goats and chickens and cows. They cook food and serve it. They fly high into the air on trapezes and perform other circus stunts.

Kids do all these jobs and more. Not all kinds of work are equally harmful. There are at least three kinds of work that no child should ever have to do. No child should work as a bonded or slave laborer, as a prostitute, or as a soldier.

BONDED LABOR

In some areas of the world, people like Iqbal's parents are so poor that they are forced to borrow money from a business owner in exchange for work that will be done in the future. For example, a family may not have enough money to feed all their children or to buy medicine. The

*Fishing platform worker
Sumatra, Indonesia*

parents might accept some money from a factory owner. In exchange, they promise that one of their children will work at the factory to pay back the money. The child works until the loan is paid back. But the child's pay is extremely low, and the child must pay for food, clothing, and shelter. The owner charges so much for these items that in many cases the loan can never be repaid. This is called bonded labor.

Being a bonded worker is like being a slave. A bonded worker is not free to leave the workplace. About 10 to 20 million children in the world are forced to work as bonded laborers. The system is most common in India, Nepal, Bangladesh, and Pakistan. Many bonded workers in these countries make carpets. They also work in stone quarries, carrying and breaking stones. In Indonesia, workers are held captive on

Stone quarry worker
Nepal

fishing platforms far out at sea for many months.

Bijay Tamang, a 13-year-old boy from Sindhupalchowk, Nepal, has worked in a carpet factory in Chabel, Nepal, for two years. He is working to pay back money that was supposed to have been loaned to his parents. But the money never reached them. A middleman, who was supposed to deliver the money, pocketed it instead. Nonetheless, Bijay became a bonded laborer—bonded by the responsibility to pay the factory the money he and his father never received.

At the factory, Bijay weaves carpets from five in the morning until midnight. He gets a meal of rice and lentils twice a day. His fingers have been badly cut. The three middle fingers of his left hand were cut deep to the bone. Threads get caught inside the cuts while he is weaving, causing him terrible pain and preventing the wounds from healing.

Some children regard bonding as a rite of passage, an event that will transform them into adults. Irfana, a twelve-year-old Pakistani girl who spent four years as a brick worker, says, "My friends and I knew that sooner or later we'd be sent off to the factories or the fields. We were tired of doing chores and minding infants. We looked forward to the day when we'd be given responsibilities and the chance to earn money."

PROSTITUTION

Another kind of work that hurts children is prostitution—sex for money. In the United States, 200,000 to 300,000 children work in

the sex trade. In India, adolescent boys and girls work in brothels in big cities such as Bombay and Calcutta. In India and Nepal, an estimated 200,000 young women have been kidnapped and sold to brothels. If they refuse to serve a customer, they are tortured.

The sex business flourishes in Thailand. A police raid in Bangkok led to the rescue of 23 girls who had been forced into prostitution. The owner of the brothel and his wife were arrested. One of the girls told about her experience in the brothel: "One time I refused to sleep with a man and they slapped me, hit me with a cane and bashed my head against the wall. One of my friends tried to run away but unfortunately she was caught and very badly beaten."

SOLDIERS AT WAR

Most children who fight in wars are forced into military service, but many volunteer to fight alongside their parents. The United Nations reports that children have been involved in wars in 25 nations in recent years. Some places torn by wars and conflicts include Rwanda, Bosnia/Herzegovina, Mozambique, Angola, Liberia, Somalia,

Afghanistan, Iran, Cambodia, and Haiti. About 200,000 children—mostly boys—serve as soldiers around the world. Most of these children are fighting in African countries.

Although children have served as soldiers for hundreds of years, the development of light, easy-to-use weapons has made it easier for armies to use children. Armies and guerrilla factions recruit children because they do not demand high salaries and do not question orders.

A human rights worker in Mozambique notes, "Child soldiers are effective because they are easy to organize, and they don't ask questions. In wartime, a commander wants total submission. You get that only from a child."

Being forced into the armed services is called conscription. In recent years, children have been conscripted in El Salvador, Ethiopia, Guatemala, Myanmar (Burma), and other countries. In Mozambique, a group of guerrilla soldiers called the Renamo forced 10,000 children into service. Young people who are not willing to fight may be tortured or thrown into jail. In Liberia, a 13-year-old boy joined the rebel forces fighting in the in the country's civil war because "they said they would kill me if I didn't go."

Many children choose to join the army. They may have lost their families in war, or their families could not afford to feed them. The army offers food, clothing, and shelter. Jean-Paul, a 15-year-old boy in Zaire, said, "I joined the army to get food for my mother, my brothers and sisters. . . . The best thing about the army is they protected me from rain and cold, and I learned how to cook. But I am glad to be out. Now I can cook for myself and my friends. Maybe I can go to school and become a carpenter—I never wanted to become a soldier."

The military also provides children with a place to belong, especially if they have been orphaned. Some young people join the army to avenge the killing of family members. One seven-year-old boy whose parents were killed in Afghanistan was asked what he wanted to do in the future. He replied, "We will attack the Russians and kill all of them."

Children also fight because they have been taught that it is the right thing to do. Their families may have religious reasons for fighting or an age-old hatred of another ethnic group. In Sri Lanka, the Tamil Tigers, a fighting group in the northern part of the country, teaches children at a young age about their responsibility to become soldiers.

Children who are forced to serve as soldiers are often treated very badly. They must watch and do horrible things. Some must kill their own family members or members of their village. Many of these children cannot return home because their families are gone. They live with terrible memories and guilt about the

In Liberia, a 13-year-old boy joined the rebel forces fighting in the country's civil war because "they said they would kill me if I didn't go."

crimes they have taken part in and have witnessed.

Children who must work as soldiers suffer in many ways. The United Nations Children's Fund (Unicef) believes that no child under the age of 18 should be recruited into the military. Children are also protected under many international laws, such as the 1989 Convention on the Rights of the Child. Despite these laws, preventing the problem is extremely difficult.

why

do

kids

WORK?

Leather worker
Dhaka, Bangladesh

IF THEY HAD A CHOICE, kids would not spend their days bent over a carpet loom or shaping brick after brick under the hot sun or stitching pieces of leather together in a dark, stuffy room. Compared to these hard jobs, school seems like a privilege, an opportunity—a pretty good way to pass the day.

Parents, too, do not easily or willingly send their children off to work. "Only the most patronizing assume that somehow parents in Asia would prefer to keep their children at work instead of school," notes one writer. In most parts of the world, children work because their families need money to buy food and clothing. Most parents who allow their young children to work feel forced into that position.

Abdul Wazel, his wife, Aklima, and their daughter, Parbin, 12, left their village near the Bay of Bengal, in Bangladesh, after a river changed course and flooded their fields. Now they live in a shantytown in Dhaka, the capital of Bangladesh. Every day Aklima and Parbin work up to 14 hours in a garment sweatshop, trimming threads and carrying fabric. "Children shouldn't have to work," Aklima says. "But if she didn't, we'd go hungry."

Although poverty forces parents to send their children to work, child labor also *increases* poverty. For every child who works, there may be an adult who cannot find a job. Children are usually paid less than adult workers—sometimes only one-third of what adults earn. As a result, adult workers' wages stay low or go down.

When parents cannot find jobs, they are more likely to send their children to work. They have more children in the hope of increasing their income. Each generation of poor, uneducated child workers becomes the next generation of poor parents who must send their kids to work. Then the cycle of poverty and illiteracy continues.

Abul Fayez and his son, Bilal Hossain, also came to Dhaka, Bangladesh, after a flood. They are among the scores of people who sit on the sidewalks breaking bricks into gravel. It is cheaper to have humans do this kind of work than to buy machines. Bilal is nine or ten years old (nobody is sure). He squats next to his father, pulling bricks from a pile and smashing them with quick blows of his hammer. They start work at 6:00 A.M. and finish about 12 hours later. For a day's work, Bilal and his father together make about 85 cents, barely enough to buy two meals of rice and vegetables.

"If I could earn more myself, I wouldn't have to bring Bilal to help me," Abul says. "But without him, we wouldn't make enough to survive."

In many countries, large numbers of children do not go to school. In some regions of the world, fewer than half of all children finish elementary school. Even if school is available and free, a family might not be able to afford school supplies, uniforms, or books.

Construction worker
Kathmandu, Nepal

*Stone quarry worker
near Delhi, India*

Animal herders, Rajasthan, India

Some families feel that a child is better off learning a trade than going to school because jobs for well-educated people may be hard to find. What's more, the child who goes to school is not helping meet the family's immediate needs.

Large families are more likely to put some of the kids to work. The more mouths there are to feed, the more money is needed. If one or both parents have died or left, the remaining family members have a harder time surviving. For example, 12-year-old Mainya Shrestha is an orphan. She lives with her brother and sister-in-law in

Lalitapur, Nepal. From five in the morning until nine at night, she works as a carpet weaver in a local factory. Mainya has been working since she was eight years old. She doesn't know any other way of living.

Religious beliefs and ethnic prejudice may also contribute to child labor. In many countries, ethnic or religious minorities face discrimination. They may find it difficult to get an education or decent jobs.

In some religions, people believe that their role in life is determined by God. In India, for example, the Hindu religion traditionally divided people into different castes. People have certain roles or occupations based on their caste. India's caste system has weakened over the last 50 years, but it still affects people's attitudes about work.

Mukti Ashram is a rehabilitation center in New Delhi for Indian boys who have been rescued from work bondage. Nearly all the children who come to Mukti Ashram are from illiterate, low-caste families. "When we ask the children: 'Who has caused this discrimination against you?' they say 'God,'" says the center's director.

A landowner in Rawalpindi, Pakistan, explains why he uses children in his fields: "Children are cheaper to run than tractors and smarter than oxen."

WHAT EMPLOYERS SAY

For employers, children are less expensive and easier to control than adults. Sadique, a carpet master, tells why he likes to hire boys aged seven to ten: "[They're] wonderfully obedient—they'd work around the clock if I asked them. I hire them first and foremost because they're economical. For what I'd pay one second-class adult weaver I can get three boys, sometimes four, who can produce first-class rugs in no time."

A landowner in Rawalpindi, Pakistan, explains why he uses children in his fields: "Children are cheaper to run than tractors and smarter than oxen."

Child Labor through History

Children have always worked. They helped out on farms and in the fields. At home, they looked after younger brothers and sisters and helped with cooking and other chores. In many cultures, a child learned a trade or craft by working alongside an adult.

From the time of the Roman Empire (circa 20 B.C.–A.D. 476) and continuing into the 1600s, many children were sold as slaves. They toiled at miserable jobs for no money. In 1212, thousands of boys and girls joined the Children's Crusade, a Christian movement to gain the Holy Land (Palestine) from the Muslims. Many crusaders, most under age 12, were kidnapped and sold into slavery in North Africa.

The first laws that regulated the work of children were passed in Venice, Italy, in 1284. These laws did not allow children to work at some of the most dangerous jobs in glass factories.

Children prospecting
for gold, circa 1850s

The world of work changed radically in England during the 1700s. Because of new inventions, machines, and technology, work moved from farms, homes, and small shops to factories and cities. These shifts continued through the early 1800s and spread to other countries, including the United States.

Factories needed many workers. Adults who took the jobs were poorly paid, so parents began sending their kids to work to increase the family's earnings. Children went to work in cotton mills, pottery factories, coal mines, food canneries, and glass factories. They also found work as chimney sweeps, newsboys and girls, and crop workers.

In 1767, shortly before the Revolutionary War in the United States, the governor of New York proudly noted that every home had a child ready to work at spinning thread. In 1832, almost 40 percent of factory workers in New England were children. As late as 1920, almost 125,000 children were working in New York City.

Some states passed laws that limited the number of hours or kinds of work children could do. It was not until 1938 that the first nationwide law about child labor was passed in the United States. This law, known as the Fair Labor Standards Act, set a minimum age and standards for employment.

Silk spinner
Kanchipuram, India

Making sesame seed oil, Jodphur, India

Employers who hire children say the kids are learning useful skills. But most jobs held by children are simple, and the child repeats the same task for the entire day. For example, a child might be asked to cut the threads off shirt buttons for 12 hours a day.

Some employers and government officials say there is nothing wrong with making children work. They say that people in different parts of the world view the process of growing up in different ways.

Imran Malik, a carpet exporter in Lahore, Pakistan, says, "For thousands of years children have worked alongside their parents in their villages. The work they now do in factories and workshops is an extension of this tradition, and in most ways an improvement on it." But children in Pakistan seldom worked apart from their families until the 1960s, when the government launched a program to expand the nation's carpet exports.

what

happens

to kids

WHO WORK?

Metalworker
Madras, India

CHILDREN WHO WORK are at risk for health problems such as injuries, stunted growth, and many diseases. Studies show that working children are hurt more easily and more seriously than adults. Many working children also endure harsh punishment from their employers. They may be beaten, burned, or thrashed. They rarely get enough sleep or food. "I never had a full meal the past three years, though we were put to work from dawn till night," says Gholad Sada, a ten-year-old carpet worker.

In a factory in Pakistan, children aged five to ten make soccer balls by hand, earning just over a dollar a day. They work 80 hours a week. They are forbidden to speak, and their eyes strain in the darkness. They have one 30-minute meal break each day. If they fall asleep, they are punished. They are also punished if their workbenches are sloppy, if they make mistakes, or if they complain. Punishment is delivered in a storage closet, where the children are hung upside down, starved, caned, or lashed.

Children and teenagers work in a world that is designed for adults. In restaurants, counters are high. In wood shops, tools are too large for small hands. A child who drives a tractor may not be able to reach the brake pedal. Safety gloves used to protect an adult's hands from dangerous chemicals fall off a child's small hands.

Metalworker
Madras, India

Every type of job presents a different set of dangers. Children are often hired to weave carpets. Shop owners say they need a child's "nimble fingers" to tie the thousands of tiny knots that make a fine carpet. But the hands of young carpet workers are covered with cuts, calluses, and scars. Their fingers are gnarled from the repetitive work. These workers often develop skin diseases. Their spines are curved from sitting in front of a loom day after day. They often have trouble breathing because of asthma, a lung disease.

"My body used to ache, sitting on the narrow hard wooden bench for hours on end," a six-year-old carpet worker says. "My fingers were sore and my thumb often got injured by the knife."

Weaver's hand
Kathmandu, Nepal

Market vendor, Dhaka, Bangladesh

Brickworker
Madras, India

Young brickworkers carry large loads of bricks on their heads. Each brick weighs almost three pounds, and a child might carry as many as 2,000 bricks in a day. The workers walk barefoot across dusty, dry brickyards. If a brick falls, it can seriously injure the worker's foot. The children also breathe in a lot of dust from the dry bricks and sand. Breathing in dust over a long period of time causes scarring of the lungs (silicosis). Silicosis leads to early death. Brickworkers also may get tuberculosis, another disease of the lungs.

Young people who work in deep-sea fishing are forced to live and work on small platforms built on stilts far out in the ocean. The platforms are full of huge holes, and it is easy to slip and fall through. Many of the children don't know how to swim. If they fall into the sea, they may drown.

Sumina, age 13, works at a furniture factory in Tangerang, Indonesia. She works in the "rubbing unit," where children sand wood to make it smooth. "The working conditions are very bad," she says. "The room is hot and the dust from rubbing is very severe. We breathe it every day. The company does not provide workers with masks. I feel confused but have nowhere to go for alternative employment. . . . I frequently suffer from fever, cough, and influenza."

In the United States, working children and adolescents account for more than 30,000 injuries and 100 deaths each year. Injuries include back and neck strains, cuts, burns, and occasionally, broken bones or amputations. Jobs in restaurants may be dangerous because of the risk of burns. Farm workers risk serious injury from heavy machines. Kids who sell newspapers on busy street corners dodge between cars to collect money.

Fishing platform worker
Sumatra, Indonesia

Chicken farmer, Sumatra, Indonesia

Leather worker
Dhaka, Bangladesh

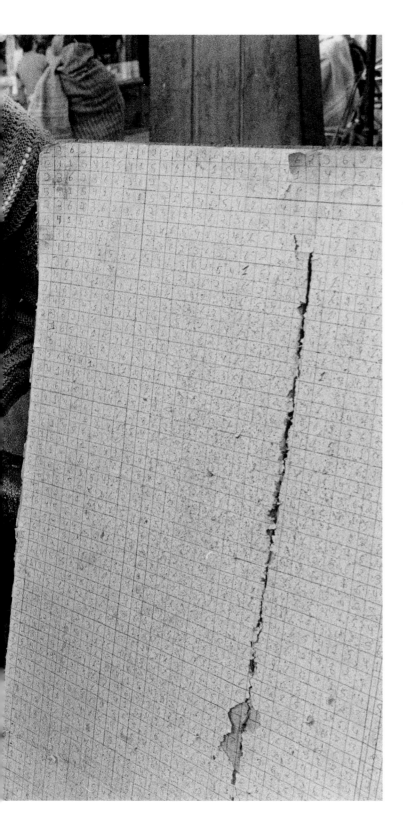

Street gamblers
Kathmandu, Nepal

STOLEN DREAMS

Working children often lose much more than their health. They lose the chance to attend school, and the opportunities school brings. Some of them lose their families. Kids who work don't have time to play, to run around and act silly, and to dream about their future. They lose their childhoods.

Doi, 13, works more than 12 hours a day in a factory in Bangkok, Thailand, making leather handbags. The factory employs 200 children to cut, sew, and glue the leather.

"My father died and my mother just didn't have enough money to feed all my brothers and sisters, so that's why I came [to Bangkok]," Doi says. "What I really miss is games. We don't have any time to play any

71

Street vendor, New Delhi, India

football (soccer) or Ta-kraw or anything like that. We work so hard. I don't understand why we can't have some time in the evening to play. I suppose it's because there's so much work to do."

Prem Magar is an 11-year-old carpet weaver in Kathmandu, Nepal. Prem and his parents used to live on a small farm, and Prem was able to go to school. But now he and his parents work in a carpet factory. Prem works 16 hours a day. He misses going to school. "I did not mind looking after cattle before and after school and working as a farm laborer during holidays," he says. "I did not mind going hungry now and then as long as I could go to school."

Bubble soap vendor
Calcutta, India

A Ragpicker's Story

*Pramila lives in Kathmandu, Nepal. She grew up in the slums and began scavenging trash for money. She tells what her life was like.**

My father walked out on my mother two months before I was born. When I was not even two, we were thrown out of the house because my mother could not pay the rent. I started working when I was six. I learned to scavenge from the ragpicker boys who came to the riverbank to look for pieces of plastic. I had to fend for myself. My mother went without food or she would just have some tea. Only in the evenings could we eat rice, but not always. So I had to buy food out of my own earnings. I woke up with the sun and went to scavenge.

There is one incident that happened to me those days that I will never forget. One day I went before dawn to Soaltee Lane to look for empty beer cans, bottles, and food in the garbage containers that had been thrown away by the nearby Hotel Soaltee Oberoi. I climbed into the container and searched for the things I had come for. I was disappointed when I could not find anything. When I jumped down in haste, I stepped on a broken piece of glass. I slashed my left foot badly as I was not wearing any slippers. When I stared at my foot with the blood gushing out, I felt nauseous. I sat down, and out of fear and pain, I began to cry. I tried to tear off a piece of cloth to bind the cut, but the skirt I was wearing was of old polyester and would not tear. I tried to stop the blood but it just gushed out from in between my fingers. I felt so helpless and I thought I was dying.

It was just about morning, and some people were passing by. A man stopped and gave me a note of 2 rupees. "Go get medicine for yourself," he said. The sight of the money made me realize how hungry I was. I had not eaten anything the night before. I stood up. I put a piece of newspaper over my bleeding foot and walked to a shop on my toe. I bought a cup of tea for myself. I did not go to the medical shop because I felt the hunger more than the pain.

*The photograph shown here is not Pramila, whose story is told, but a girl of about the same age doing the same kind of work in Dhaka, Bangladesh. Pramila's story is excerpted from Voice of Child Workers (Jan.–Apr. 1993) and is used with permission.

Susana Vasquez is 17 years old and lives in Salisbury, Maryland. She was born in Mexico and immigrated to the United States with her family when she was seven years old. When she was nine years old, she began working in the fields as a migrant farmworker. This is what she says about that time:

"I know what it is like for a thirsty child to work under the hot sun on 90-degree days. I know what it is like for a child who is cold to work on rainy days that make the fields muddy and difficult to work in. On those days I remember getting home all wet and caked with mud. The mud made my shoes very heavy. What I don't know, however, is what it is like to be invited to a birthday party or to play with other girls my age. I had no time for playing house, going to the movies, watching cartoons, or doing homework."

Too much work, too many hours, physically demanding work, terrible working conditions—clearly, these situations hurt children. That is why governments around the world have passed laws to ban child labor and why many people are seeking to put an end to this suffering.

Robbed of their dreams, their time to play, many working kids still hold on to their hope. They make friends with other workers. Like Iqbal Masih, they fight for what they know is right. They find ways to survive.

A former bonded worker in India, a 10-year-old boy, says, "Among us there were children who spoke Nepali, Bhutani, Bangia, and other languages which we could not understand. Yet our common problems and aims bound us together and we became good friends."

Susana Vasquez, the migrant worker, says, "I am not ashamed of the work I did. Instead, I feel more mature and stronger than other girls my age. I feel older than 17 because I have a long history behind me. I appreciate what my parents have done to make it in the United States."

what

can

be

DONE?

Brickworker
Kathmandu, Nepal

ALL OF US, as members of the world community, cannot afford to ignore the suffering of children who must work in harmful situations. Many people are looking for ways to put an end to child labor. Unfortunately, there are no easy answers. It's not as simple as passing a law. Solutions must bring together a number of approaches.

Almost every nation in the world has laws that limit the amount and types of work children can do. In most countries, children must be at least 14 or 15 years old to work; in about 30 countries the minimum age is 12 or 13.

Newsboy
Chicago, United States

Know Your Rights

Having a job can be a rewarding experience. Many kids like to earn money to buy things or to start a savings program. A job can give you a sense of responsibility, teach you useful skills, and help you figure out what you might want to do later in life. But if you work too much, your health, grades, and social life may suffer.

If you have a job, whether it's part-time or full-time, you should understand your rights as a worker and learn about laws governing young workers. In the United States, these laws are part of the Fair Labor Standards Act and the Occupational Safety and Health Administration Act (OSHA Act). If you live in the United States, you must be at least 14 years old to have a job. Exceptions to the minimum age are made for newspaper delivery, farm work, and acting.

Besides the minimum age requirement, child labor laws set many other limits. There are laws governing when and how many hours a young person may work. Many jobs are prohibited for young people, such as welding, driving a truck, and serving liquor. The Fair Labor Standards Act also prevents young people from operating most kinds of machines. The OSHA Act sets minimum standards for workplace safety and health.

For information about the labor laws that affect children and adolescents, you can contact the labor department in your state. Most labor departments have a section that enforces labor laws. You may also contact the Wage and Hour Division of the U.S. Department of Labor.

Sadly, despite laws and guidelines, child labor continues. The laws are ignored or broken. Sometimes the laws are vague or riddled with loopholes. There may not be enough people to inspect factories and other workplaces to make sure labor laws are followed. Labor inspectors may be poorly paid and trained, or factory owners may bribe the inspectors, paying them not to report any violations of the law.

Because child labor laws by themselves often do not work, a broader approach is needed. Ideally, better jobs and wages would be available for more people in poor countries. People who study the child labor problem also suggest many other solutions:

➤ Increase the opportunity for *free public education*. Agencies such as the International Labour Organisation (ILO) and Unicef (the United Nations Children's Fund) focus on education as the cornerstone of progress. "With very, very few exceptions, no nation in the world today is too poor to provide free primary education for its children," says Assefa Bequele, a child labor expert for the ILO.

When a state requires education for all children, the number of working children falls. In much of India, primary education is not required. But in the Indian state of Kerala, where children are required to go to school, child labor is reduced. Governments can also make sure that schools provide free uniforms, books, and meals to students. This takes some of the burden off families.

Garbage picker
Jodhpur, India

Agricultural worker, Kathmandu, Nepal

Market vendor
Acapulco, Mexico

➤ Identify regions with the largest number of working children as targets for *development assistance,* including help in finding jobs for adults.

➤ *Improve the status of women and girls* to help keep them from being exploited in the workplace. In 1994, the World Conference on Population and Development recommended giving high priority to programs and policies to assist women and girls.

➤ Put in place an *adult minimum wage* and allow adults and children to participate in *trade unions* to protest low wages and poor working conditions. Adult workers who have the right to negotiate for a living wage do not have to send their children to work.

➤ Countries should work to *respect the internationally recognized rights of workers.* For example, slavery, bonded labor, and using children as soldiers violate basic human rights.

➤ *Increase enforcement of child labor laws* by providing more labor inspectors with better training and pay.

➤ Empower working children and their families by encouraging development of *self-help organizations for the poor* to make them aware of their rights. Local communities and national and international organizations can join forces to advocate an end to child labor and to inform workers of their rights and the possibilities for a better life.

Market vendor, St. Paul, United States

Beggar
Jakarta, Indonesia

Beggars, Bombay, India

*School sponsored
by the International
Labour Organisation
Madras, India*

HUMAN RIGHTS GROUPS

Hundreds of international and national organizations, such as the ILO, Unicef, and the Child Labor Coalition, are trying to improve the lives of working children. In India, the South Asian Coalition on Child Servitude (SACCS) was founded in 1989 by Kailash Satyarthi to combat child labor, especially bonded labor. Satyarthi raids factories to rescue young bonded workers. He has organized rallies of Indian children freed from bonded labor.

Another group working in Pakistan is the Bonded Labor Liberation Front (BLLF), founded in 1988 by Essan Ulla Khan, the man who helped rescue Iqbal Masih. BLLF has led the fight against bonded labor, liberating 30,000 adults and children from brick factories, carpet factories, and farms. BLLF has placed 11,000 children in its own school system. BLLF legal advisers draft legal complaints against factories, and other staff members inform workers of their rights.

Brickworker
Madras, India

Carpet factory owners have criticized BLLF in newspaper stories. BLLF headquarters were raided and their equipment was stolen. The Pakistani government charged Essan Ulla Khan with sedition and economic treason, crimes punishable by death. He is exiled in Europe. "They will jail me if I return to Pakistan," he says.

BOYCOTTS

If you live in a country where child labor is not widespread, you might wonder if there's anything you can do. Many people in Europe, Canada, and the United States do not want to buy products made by children. But consumers don't always know who made the things they buy. When people learn that kids made a product, they are often angry. They stop buying the product. They may even organize a boycott, asking others not to buy it.

One program that many U.S. and European consumers have embraced is called Rugmark. In India, Pakistan, and Nepal, carpets made without child labor have a label that says Rugmark. This tells the buyer that no child worked on the rug. One percent of the price of the carpet goes toward a Unicef program to educate former child workers.

Some American and European companies have demanded that their overseas factories stop using child workers. In 1995, bowing to public pressure, many importers in the U.S., Sweden, Italy, Great Britain, France, and Germany stopped ordering carpets from Pakistan.

In India, Pakistan, and Nepal, carpets made without child labor have a label that says Rugmark. This tells the buyer that no child worked on the rug.

But some child labor experts, including the global charity Oxfam, say that boycotts and other measures taken against factories that hire kids can hurt more than they help. "Any anti-trade action is quite damaging, since trade is one of the most important engines of economic growth," says child labor expert Assefa Bequele.

In addition, international boycotts don't affect most child workers. Only a small number of Asia's child workers are in industries that sell products to other countries. The vast majority work in small, local businesses, far beyond the reach of trade sanctions and boycotts.

WHAT ARE COUNTRIES DOING?

No matter how tricky the problem of child labor is, it must be tackled. In the United States, Senator Tom Harkin (Democrat from

Restaurant worker
Jodhpur, India

Iowa) has sponsored bills that would prevent U.S. companies from importing products made by children. He has also worked with international organizations to find ways to end the cycle of poverty in which working children are trapped.

In India, former prime minister P. V. Narasimha Rao set a goal of freeing two million children from work by the year 2000. A government incentive plan pays parents a monthly stipend and food rations if they send their children to school instead of to work.

Hong Kong has been very successful in controlling child labor. In 1980, school became a requirement for children under age 15. The government also began to inspect factories regularly to make sure no young children were working. In 1986, for example, there were more than 250,000 factory inspections. Social programs also helped parents so that they didn't have to send their kids to work.

In Brazil, the government joined with Unicef to create a program to help street children. Local volunteers, supported by government agencies, work to get kids off the street.

THE FUTURE

The costs of allowing kids to go to work instead of school are great. In an increasingly complex world, it is important for people to be able to read, write, and do math. Without education, people have fewer options in life. They have little choice of what work they can do. They may not know their rights.

As the gap between the rich and the poor grows in many parts of the world, children will continue to be seen as a source of extra money for their families and as cheap workers for employers. In the United States, the number of young workers is growing.

The rights of parents and the rights of children are not easy to define. There's no clear way to end child labor. That doesn't mean there's nothing you can do. Lots of kids have found ways to become involved.

kids

speak out

against

CHILD LABOR

American students in Quincy, Massachusetts, meet Iqbal Masih.

ALTHOUGH IQBAL MASIH only lived to the age of 12, he made a difference in the world. He fought against a system that was wrong. He spoke out against child labor. When Iqbal's story was told in America and Europe, many kids learned for the first time about the difficult lives of working children in different parts of the world. They got mad. They wanted to help.

In 1994, a group of seventh-grade students at Broad Meadows Middle School in Quincy, Massachusetts, met Iqbal Masih. He came to their school to talk about bonded child labor. Iqbal told the students that he wanted to be the Abraham Lincoln of his country, who would free children trapped in factories. He told them he wanted to start a school in his village for kids like him.

Iqbal was killed just a few months after he visited the U.S. The students at Broad Meadows School decided to raise money to build the school Iqbal had dreamed of starting. They sent out thousands of letters, fliers, and faxes, and they set up a web site about Iqbal called "A Bullet Can't Kill a Dream." They came to school early, stayed late, and worked through vacations. By September 1996, the students had raised $123,000 from people in all 50 states and 20 other countries.

The money will establish the Iqbal Masih Education Center, a school for 200 poor Pakistani children who have been bonded workers or are at risk of being sold. It will also provide money to 50 Pakistani families to buy back their kids from bonded labor.

Another group of kids, in Minneapolis, Minnesota, acted in a play about Iqbal called "The Spirit of Iqbal."

In Ontario, Canada, 12-year-old Craig Kielburger read about the murder of Iqbal and decided to do something. He formed an activist group called Free the Children and started speaking at schools across Canada.

"We Americans tend to expect very little of our children. We expect them to be spoiled and cynical. We allow them to be precocious in some ways and babies in others. Then we criticize them for being shallow and selfish. The students from Quincy should make us think again. They were not moved by Iqbal because he had the glamor of a rock singer or sports hero or movie star—malnutrition had stunted his growth and his back was crooked from bending over the loom. They recognized his heroism and responded to that. Our young people want to do more; they want us to expect more of them."

—Albert Shanker, former president,
American Federation of Teachers

Working after school, Craig and his classmates put together information packets and circulated petitions. In December 1995, Craig traveled to India, Pakistan, Bangladesh, Nepal, and Thailand to see for himself what life was like for kids working in those places.

"It's made a complete difference in the way I see things," Craig said after the trip. "I'm not rich, but I'm not struggling either. But people over there are struggling. And that's one of the reasons I feel so strongly."

What follows are statements by kids who are speaking out against child labor. They are adding their voices to the many others, young and old, who want to find a way to make life better for people across the world.

Dear Mr. President:

I am a sixth-grader at the Friends School of Minnesota. In our class, we are learning about child labor. I am appalled at the fact that American companies are allowed to buy clothes and other products from factories in third world countries where children work for as low as $.33 an hour. They work 13-hour shifts and sometimes are called for a 23-hour shift. They can't go to school when they hold jobs. They have to go to work, otherwise their families could starve. I think that I, as a citizen, can help stop this by not buying from companies that have factories in countries that use child labor. I also think that you as a president can help stop this mess by making laws to regulate importing of child-labor made products.

Ben Birnbaum
Minneapolis, Minnesota

> For once I am aware that our country and this world is so big, yet the plight of children of poor parents is the same everywhere.
>
> *Mohan, 10-year-old freed bonded worker from India*

One night my dad came home from work very excited. He said that there was going to be an episode of *Turning Point* on television about a great man named Kailash Satyarthi. We sat down together and watched the program, which was filmed during one of Kailash's raids of a rug factory using bonded child labor. I was absolutely horrified by the small rooms of rug looms, the small pot of rice the children had to eat from, and, most of all, by the confused children themselves. I cannot fully express how I felt during the program, but my heart filled with sorrow for the kids. That was when I knew I had to do something to help.

I think the best way to get other teenagers involved with building up opposition to bonded child labor is through education. We are the consumers of tomorrow. If you educate us, then we will educate others. I believe that kids have a great influence on their parents. If the child tells his or her parents, "I don't want products made by child labor," I believe the adults will listen and take action.

Shannon Goold
Falls Church, Virginia

I am concerned because children my age and younger are working in hazardous areas, while I am out having fun with my friends. I could be enjoying myself at the movies or eating out while children around the world are working 16-hour days, trying to fill my needs by making the clothes I wear or the glasses I drink out of.

We can stop child labor by speaking out to schools and getting kids interested in helping. We can run fund-raisers and protests for kids as well as their parents to get the message across that they can help. I feel that if more kids get interested we can make more of a difference than adults. Although we are younger and not as experienced as most adults, we do have the power to imagine what children our ages are feeling as they work.

We can ask our parents to stop buying goods made by children. We don't want to wear clothes made by kids. We don't want to play with toys made by kids. We want the children to be free.

Elizabeth Carter
Falls Church, Virginia

We are glad that people in many places have started knowing our plight and are working to help us. Surely, one day child servitude will be a thing of the past.

Dillip, 10-year-old freed bonded worker from India

The youth of Connecticut mill towns, such as the one I live in, Willimantic, have an awareness and sympathy for child laborers that is informed by our own regional history. During the 19th and early 20th centuries, many of our mills employed children. So when we heard Craig Kielburger on the *Today Show,* we were moved to act.

As the school year closed, we were able to collect over 150 signatures on petitions about child labor. I know kids who usually get into trouble, don't get the best grades, and don't really care about school. Yet, they were some of the most excited ones about becoming involved and circulating the petitions. They would take two or three copies and come back at the end of the day in need of more. I even had to convince one girl not to sign it twice, since that would be illegal. As soon as she found out about child labor, she had a purpose and a mission.

Since this school year started, about a week and a half ago, about 20 kids have already come together and organized a car wash, bake sale, and a can and bottle drive, where we will not only raise money, but collect more signatures as well. We will begin a letter-writing campaign, continue our fundraising and petition drives, and look at ways to involve other kids in our state.

Dianna English
Willimantic, Connecticut

Circus worker, Madras, India